AN INTERNATIONAL AIRPORT

words: Steve McDonald

illustrations: Alan Raine

design: Ian Gwilt

British Library Cataloguing in Publication Data
McDonald, Steve
 An international airport.
 1. Airports
 I. Title II. Raine, Alan
 387.7'36

Copyright © 1990 World International Publishing Limited.
All rights reserved.
Published in Great Britain by World International Publishing Limited,
an Egmont Company, Egmont House, PO Box 111, Great Ducie Street,
Manchester M60 3BL. Printed in Italy. ISBN 0 7235 4297 X

FOREWORD

Apart from the greater distances covered (and in such short periods of time), air travel is very similar to other methods of transport. It exists to get you, the passenger and your baggage, safely and comfortably from one place to another.

Although it looks simple and straightforward, air travel is highly technical and much goes on behind the scenes. Millions of pounds and thousands of people are involved: from travel agents to air traffic controllers, airport operators to airlines.

I am pleased to see that this book manages to get behind the scenes at a typical international airport to describe just what it takes to operate a modern air transport system. It does it in terms that will be understood by the young aircraft enthusiast and the first time air traveller alike.

It is a fascinating story and well presented. Recommended reading for the next (or first?) time you fly.

Gil Thompson, O.B.E.
Chief Executive
Manchester Airport plc.

World International Publishing would like to thank all the airlines, airport authorities and other companies we have featured for their help and kind assistance in the preparation of this book, especially the following: Manchester Airport plc, Dan Air Services Ltd., Dan Air Engineering Ltd., Manchester Handling Ltd., Boeing Airplane Co., British Aerospace plc., Brian Robinson, George Ditchfield and Norman Barfield.

CONTENTS

The history of air travel 4
How an airliner flies 6
A modern airliner 8
It's easy to fly 10
Preparing for the flight – passengers and baggage 12
Preparing for the flight – the airliner 14
The airport 16
On the flight deck 18
The flight 20
Air traffic control 22
Maintenance and engineering 24
Airlines and aircraft 26
Cargo 28
Glossary 30
Airport checklist 32

THE HISTORY OF AIR TRAVEL

For centuries, one of man's greatest ambitions was to fly like the birds. If they could do it, why couldn't we? Man eventually made his first aerial ascent in 1783, even though the lighter than air balloon was unlike anything he could witness in nature. Since then, man's conquest of the air has developed at an ever increasing pace. Today we can be whisked 3,500 miles (5,600 km) from London to New York in just 2½ hours at a speed of 1,350 mph (2,160 kph) – more than twice the speed of sound.

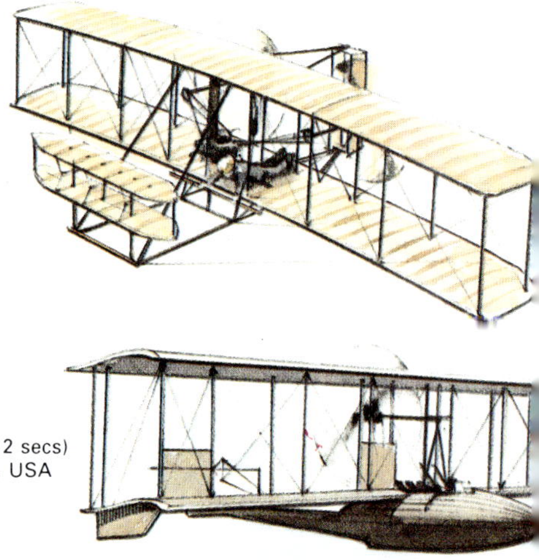

Wright Flyer I
17th December, 1903
The first successful powered aeroplane flight (120 ft (36 m)/12 secs)
Orville Wright – North Carolina, USA

de Havilland D.H.34
2nd April, 1922
The first airline to introduce air stewards (and aircraft livery)
Daimler Airways (London – Paris)

de Havilland D.H.16
7th October, 1919
The oldest airline still in service today
KLM Royal Dutch Airlines (Amsterdam – London commenced 17th May, 1920)

Armstrong Whitworth Argosy
17th December, 1922
The first airline to offer hot meals in flight
Imperial Airways (London – Paris)

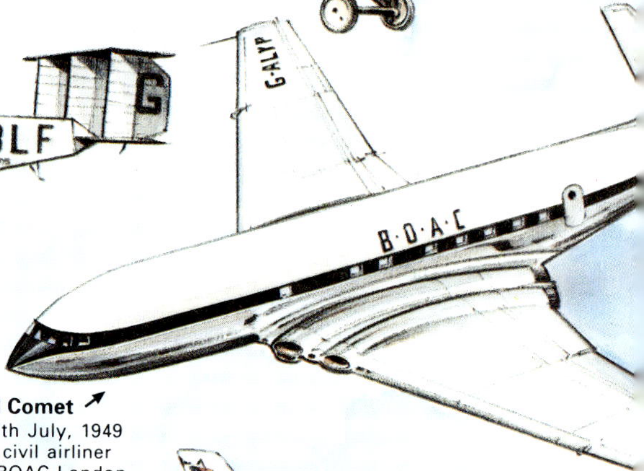

Douglas DC-3 (Dakota)
First flight 17th December, 1935
The most famous airliner in history
First service American Airlines 25th June, 1936 (over 10,000 built)

de Havilland Comet
First flight 27th July, 1949
First pure jet civil airliner
First service BOAC London – Johannesburg 2nd May, 1952

Vickers Viscount
First flight 16th July, 1948
First turbo-prop civil airliner
First service BEA London – Paris 29th July, 1950

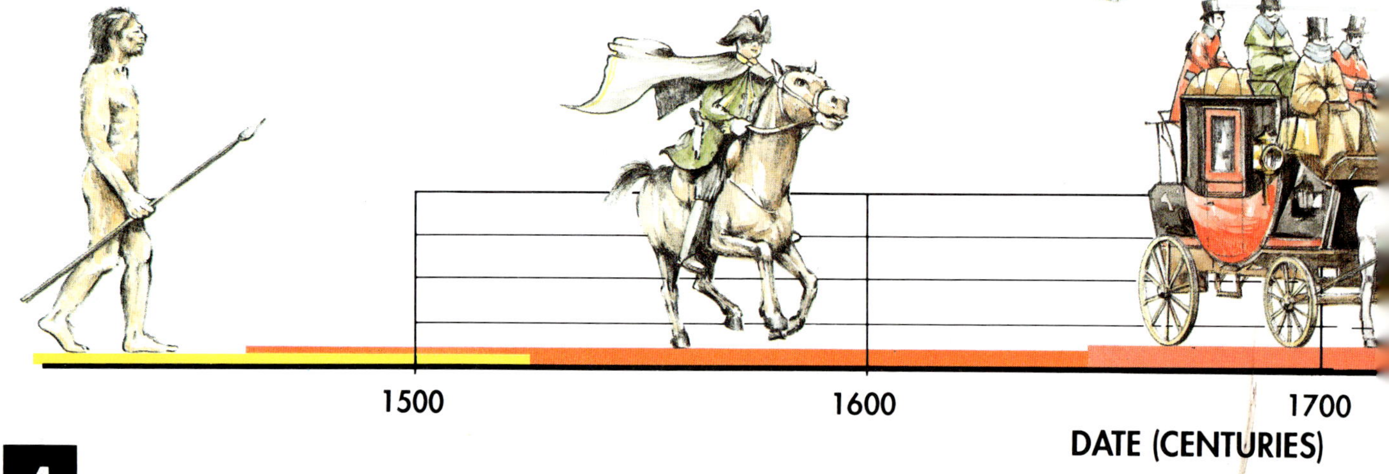

1500   1600   1700

DATE (CENTURIES)

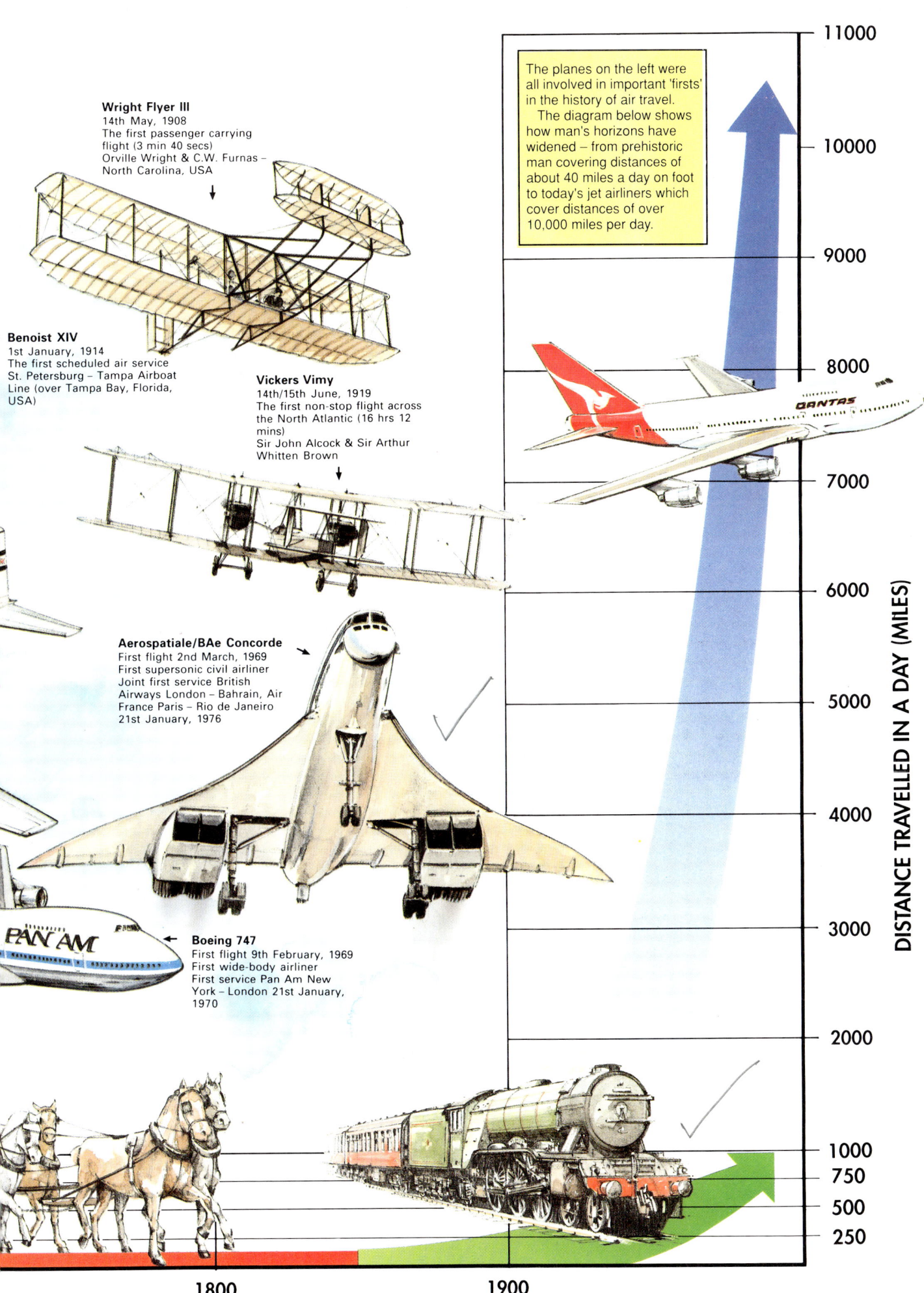

HOW AN AIRLINER FLIES

Today's airliners are designed on the same principles of flight discovered by the Wright brothers and others before them, even though they bear little resemblance to those first aircraft. Experience gained over the years means that we now know very much more about how we can build bigger and better aircraft and engines. This has enabled us to achieve incomparably greater results than the pioneers. In addition, secondary aids such as radio, radar and on-board safety equipment have made flying the safest means of travel today.

POWER PLANTS

Today's airliners are much more efficient than the old pre and post-war aircraft because they use a different type of engine. Until 1949, all airliners were powered by piston engines, just like those in today's motor cars. These are known as four stage engines. The modern jet – developed in three forms – produces continuous, rather than intermittent, power.

TURBOJET

The turbojet (or pure jet) pulls in a steady stream of air which is speeded up by being squashed through a series of small propellers called compressors, before being injected with fuel and ignited. The reaction of the exhaust gases propels the aircraft forward. The compressors are run by means of a rotating shaft linked to a turbine spun by the exhaust gases.

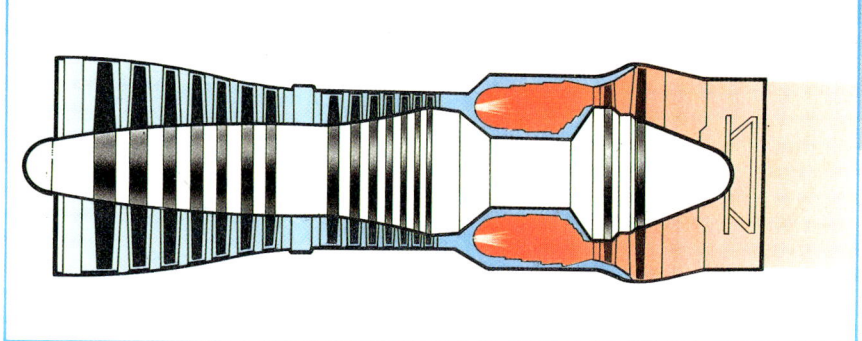

TURBOPROP

Developed from the principle of the turbojet, the turboprop incorporates extra turbines to make the jet exhaust actually turn a propeller which provides the thrust. It is much more efficient at lower heights, and therefore for shorter trips.

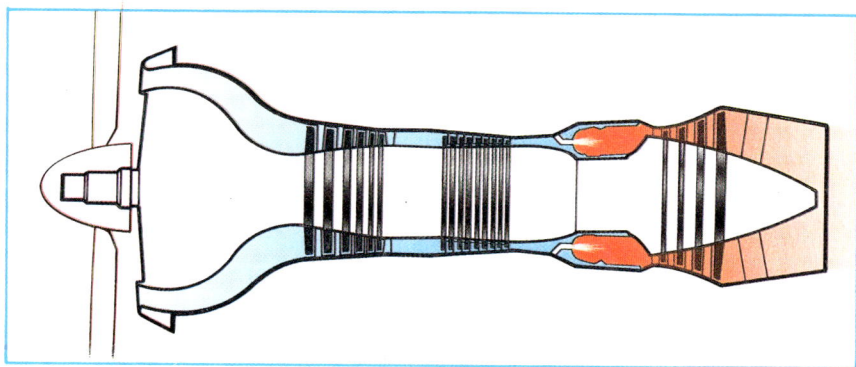

TURBOFAN

The turbofan is a big engine that powers today's jumbo jets. Developed from the turboprop, the front fan (propeller) further helps to compress the air passing through the engine. Most of the extra thrust comes from air flowing around the main engine, which also helps to reduce engine noise.

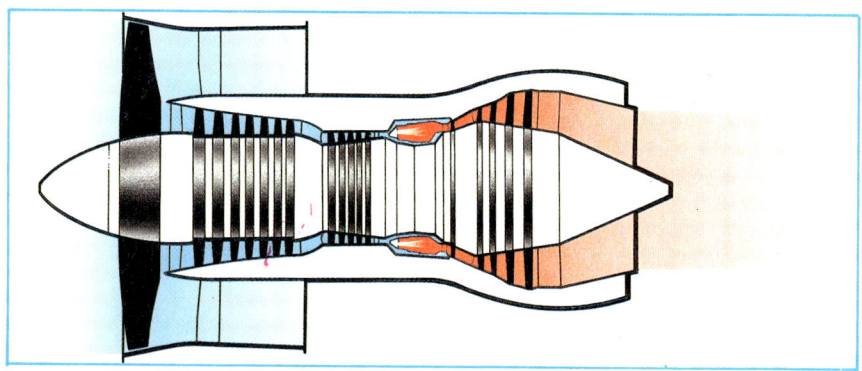

THE PRINCIPLES OF FLIGHT

It took hundreds of years for the first potential flyers to discover the principles of flight.

For an aircraft flying at a steady speed, height and direction, the forces acting on it are in balance. When any one force changes, there will be a change in the others. For example, more power gives greater thrust over drag which gives an increase in speed and, in turn, an increase in lift.

Lift is created by a difference in air pressure above and below the wing. This happens as the air passing over the top of the wing is forced to speed up as it has further to travel than the air passing below, so causing a low pressure area.

The three principle controls of an aircraft are the elevators (for nose up and down), ailerons (left or right wings up or down) and rudder (nose to left or right). Modern high speed airliners incorporate wing flaps and slats which, when closed, give a low drag wing for high speed but, when extended, greatly increase the area of lift, needed for slow descents.

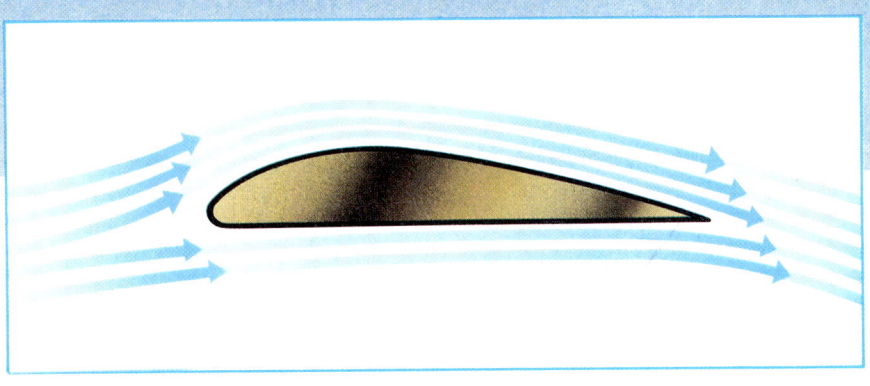

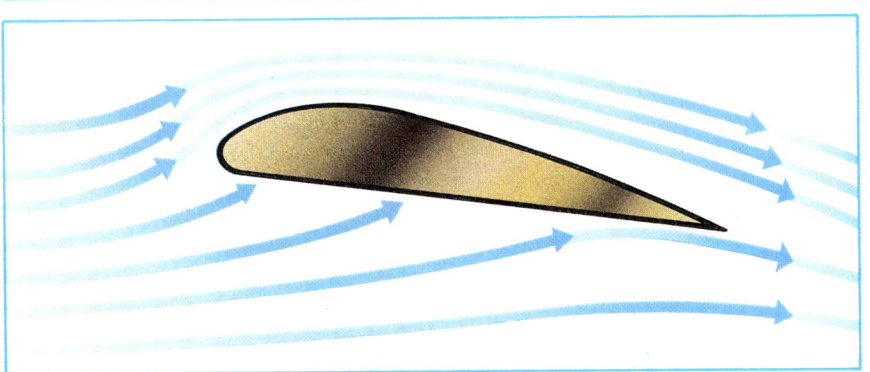

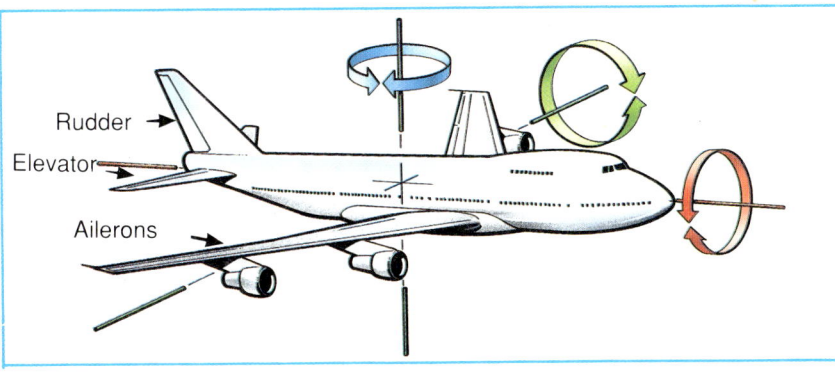

7

A MODERN AIRLINER

Although airliners appear to have changed very little in the past thirty years or so, great developments have been made in design, materials, manufacturing processes, engines and electronics. Following the introduction of the jumbo jets – starting with the Boeing 747 – airports too had to enlarge and develop their facilities to cope with the greatly increased number of passengers carried on each flight. Different aircraft are designed to do different jobs, from small propeller driven aircraft for local airports with few passengers to the supersonic Concorde for businessmen who need to travel quickly. The Boeing 757 shown here is a medium-range aeroplane which can carry up to 239 passengers over a distance of more than 3,000 miles (4,800 km).

1 Radome (housing scanners, aerials etc.)
2 Cockpit
3 1st Officer's seat
4 Pilot's seat
5 Observer's seat
6 Service door
7 Toilet
8 Galley
9 Overhead lockers
10 Aerials
11 1st class seating
12 Partition
13 Tourist class seating
14 Escape chute (in door)
15 Wing fuel tank

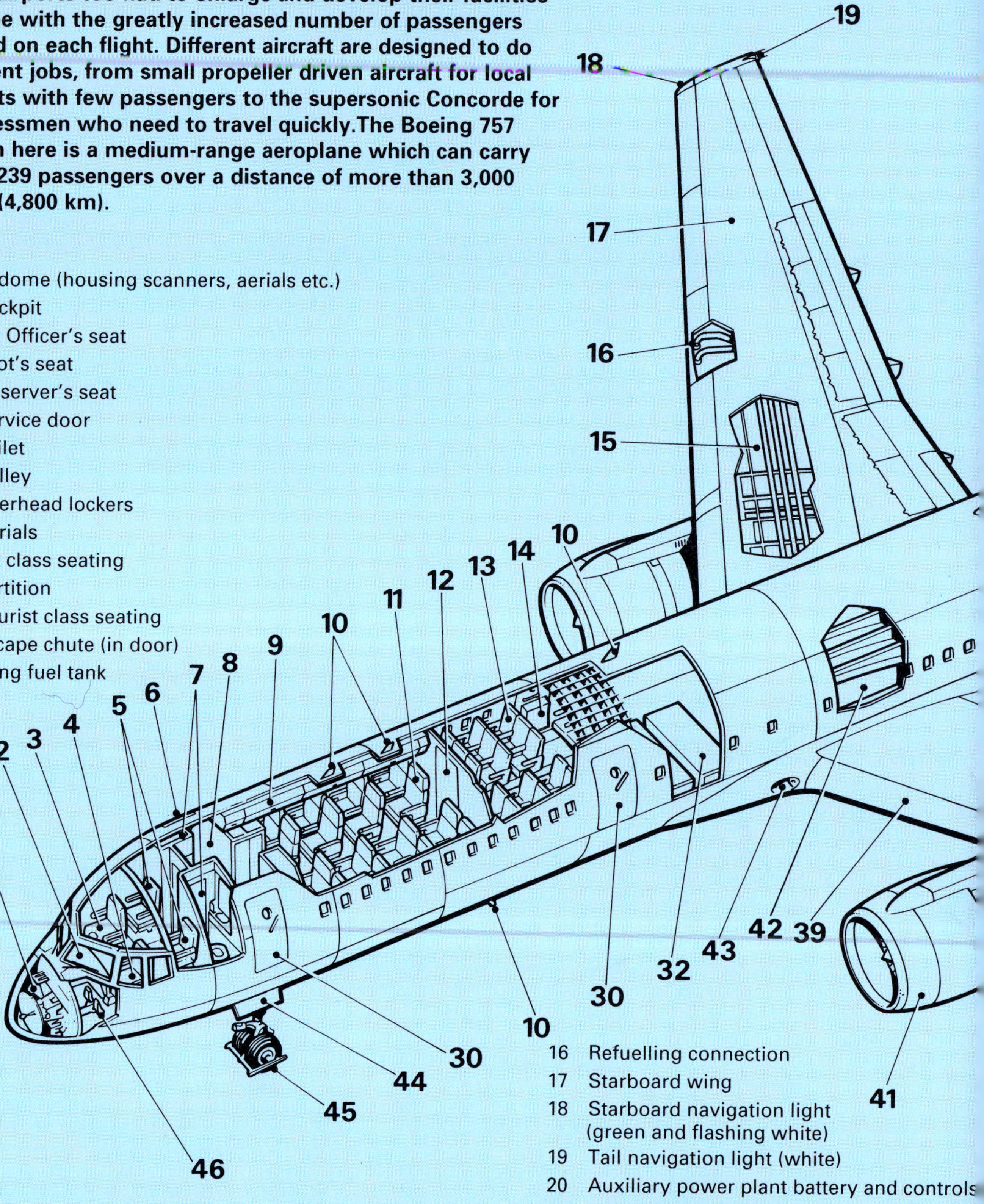

16 Refuelling connection
17 Starboard wing
18 Starboard navigation light (green and flashing white)
19 Tail navigation light (white)
20 Auxiliary power plant battery and controls
21 Life jacket (under seat)
22 Tailfin
23 Starboard tailplane

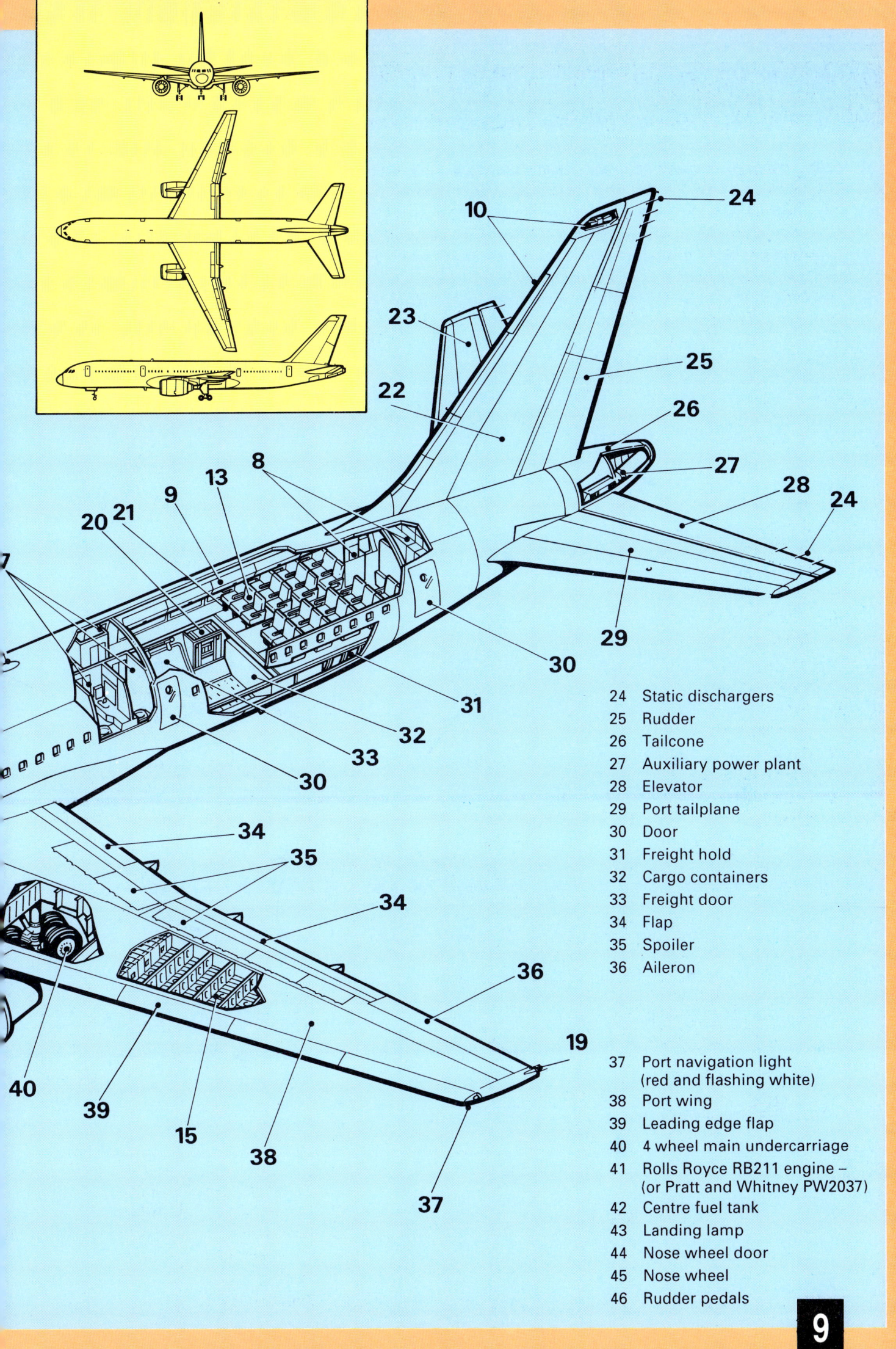

24 Static dischargers
25 Rudder
26 Tailcone
27 Auxiliary power plant
28 Elevator
29 Port tailplane
30 Door
31 Freight hold
32 Cargo containers
33 Freight door
34 Flap
35 Spoiler
36 Aileron

37 Port navigation light
   (red and flashing white)
38 Port wing
39 Leading edge flap
40 4 wheel main undercarriage
41 Rolls Royce RB211 engine –
   (or Pratt and Whitney PW2037)
42 Centre fuel tank
43 Landing lamp
44 Nose wheel door
45 Nose wheel
46 Rudder pedals

IT'S EASY TO FLY

From the very early days of commercial flying, when pilots and cabin crew first started to wear smart uniforms, a sense of mystery and excitement has surrounded air travel. But although air travel is a highly technical business, booking a ticket and getting to your destination, whether it is in the same country (known as a domestic flight) or some sun-drenched holiday resort abroad (an international flight), is surprisingly easy.

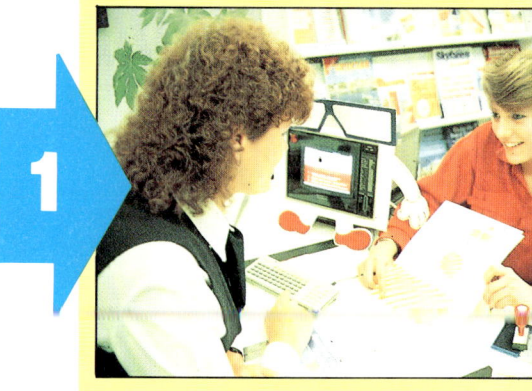

DEPARTURE HALL

Because passengers are asked to check in well before the flight is scheduled to depart, in case of any unforeseen problems, they have time to do a bit of shopping or relax with a drink or a snack before they are called to board their flight. International airports have a wide range of shops, restaurants and other facilities on hand.

CHECK-IN

Having arrived at the airport, all passengers must check in. This lets the airline know the passengers have arrived. Looking at the destination board, passengers are directed to a special desk where they show their tickets and hand over their luggage, which will be loaded into the aircraft's hold. Each passenger is given a boarding card which shows where the aircraft is parked (the 'gate') and which seat the passenger has been allocated.

THE TRAVEL AGENT

The most convenient way to book a flight is to visit your local travel agent. They will help you to sort out any problems, such as, if on holiday, where to go or the best route to travel.

SCHEDULED OR I.T.?

Airlines organize their flights in two different ways, rather like bus and coach operators. Scheduled flights operate to a fixed timetable and fly no matter how many passengers book a seat. Inclusive tours (I.T.s), however, are based on a holiday package, combining a hotel and the flight, relying on every place being booked.

THE PASSENGER TICKET

Every passenger is given a ticket/baggage check. It shows the places he is flying between, the date and time of the flights and the flight numbers. Every flight is allocated a unique flight number, which incorporates the airline's flight code.

CAR PARKING

A major international airport, like London's Heathrow, handles a staggering 38 million passengers a year. As well as organizing the airlines to fly everyone in and out, the airport authority has to provide proper facilities 'land side' (away from the aircraft operating areas) for air travellers, including car parks, bus and coach stations, taxi ranks and even railway stations. Passengers using 'off-airport' car parks are bussed to the terminal building.

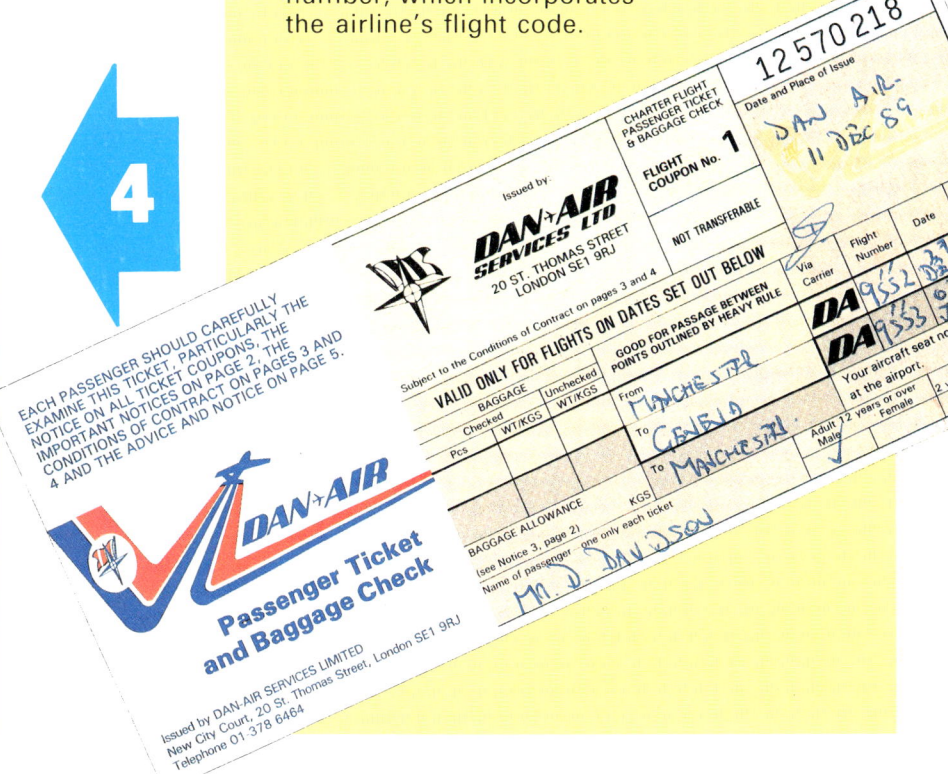

PREPARING FOR THE FLIGHT

Once the passenger has checked in with his baggage, he can relax knowing that all he has left to do is to listen for the boarding announcement. But unseen by him, he and his fellow passengers have started a flurry of behind the scenes activity that will only end when they are on board, with the doors shut and the aircraft heading down the runway to yet another take-off to yet another destination.

CREW BRIEFING
When the air crew arrive at the airport, they have to be briefed. The flight crew check the weather conditions and read the Notams (Notices for Airmen) which detail any changes to the navigational aids or airport services en route. The cabin crew check the passenger list to see who has special requirements.

LOAD SHEET
When the flight dispatcher receives the details of the flight, a load sheet is prepared. This is a legal document which shows the various loads that go to make up an aircraft's total weight and makes sure that everything is properly distributed to keep the aircraft in balance and within its maximum operating weight allowed.

AIRLINE OPERATIONS ROOM
Every airline has an operations section which schedules the aircraft in its fleet to operate the various services. When delays occur, through breakdown, air traffic control problems or bad weather, it is their responsibility to find a replacement aeroplane or make other arrangements for passengers.

Passengers and Baggage

PASSENGER CARE
Airlines take special care of their passengers, especially people who need extra help. Unaccompanied children are well looked after, severely handicapped passengers are boarded and settled before other passengers, and individual meals are prepared for passengers with special requests.

SEAT ALLOCATION
When a passenger checks in, he is asked where he would like to sit and is then given a seat number. If the aircraft is not full, the seats are allocated in such a way that the aircraft will be balanced. When the flight is closed (no more passengers will be accepted), the final passenger count is given to the flight dispatcher.

FLIGHT DISPATCHER
The flight dispatcher is responsible for making sure all the ground handling is properly completed before the aircraft is due to take off. This includes supervizing the loading of the catering, fuel, cargo and passengers, as well as completing the load sheet.

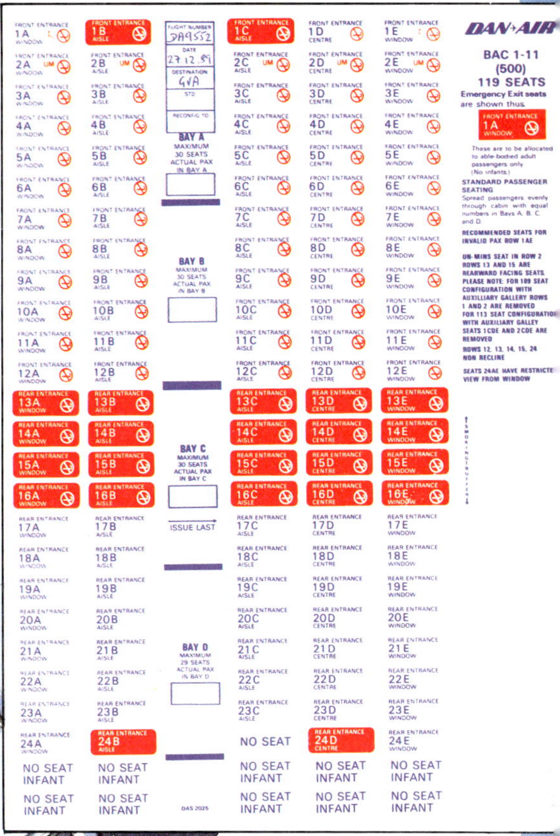

BAGGAGE HANDLING
When the passenger checks in his luggage, it is labelled with the flight number and destination before it is sent along a conveyor belt to the baggage sort hall. The bags are sorted by porters onto a line of trolleys which are taken out to the aircraft where they are loaded aboard. Modern airports, however, now barcode the luggage which is then sorted automatically.

CONTAINERS
With the large numbers of passengers carried on today's wide body airliners, airlines have introduced containerization to speed up handling and turn-round time. Metal containers designed to fit the shape of the aircraft's underfloor cargo holds are filled in the baggage sort hall and then loaded direct onto the aircraft.

PREPARING FOR THE FLIGHT

An airliner only makes money for its owners when it is in the air. Therefore, the less time it is on the ground, the more profitable it is for the airline. When an airliner lands, it has to be 'turned round' for its next flight as quickly as possible. With all services planned well before it lands, the turn-round can be completed in less than 30 minutes, although it can involve 45 people and 15 items of equipment. As you look out of the terminal building at the aircraft on which you are about to fly, the number of vehicles around it might surprise you, but they all have a very important part to play.

1 BAGGAGE AND CARGO HANDLING
In addition to the mobile conveyor belt which helps the baggage handlers to load individual personal baggage, special loading vehicles are used to load containers already filled with baggage, dramatically reducing loading time for big airliners. Many passenger airliners also carry freight in their lower fuselage holds.

10 CATERING
Meals are prepared in special catering units on or near the airport. To save space on the aircraft and minimize serving time, the meals are prepared on small trays and packed in containers. The catering vehicle is fitted with a scissor lift which allows the airport workers to unload through the service door at cabin level.

9 WATER SUPPLIES
As with every creature on this planet, we need fresh water – even when we're flying! Another vehicle to rendezvous with the airliner is the water service vehicle which provides pure water for passenger use.

8 AUXILIARY POWER SUPPLIES
An airliner's electrical power is generated when its engines are running. When it has parked and the engines shut down, lighting and power are provided either by an on-board auxiliary power unit (APU), mobile ground power generator unit or ring main provided by the airport.

7 TOW TRUCK
Aircraft park 'nose in' to make maximum use of apron space. As they can't go backwards under their own power, they need the assistance of a tow truck for 'push back' before they can start up their engines and move towards the runway. It takes a 70 ton (71 tonne) truck to move a 245 ton (250 tonne) Boeing 747.

The Airliner

2 MAINTENANCE
The pilot of the arriving flight reports anything unusual that has occurred. The airline's engineers put things right and conduct routine checks which include the engine, hydraulic systems, brakes and tyres. Only if the plane is reported to be in perfect working order will it be allowed to take off again.

3 SECURITY ✓
Customs officers check the stocks of on-board duty free goods on the airliner and make sure no smuggling has taken place, while the airport police and security forces maintain vigilance.

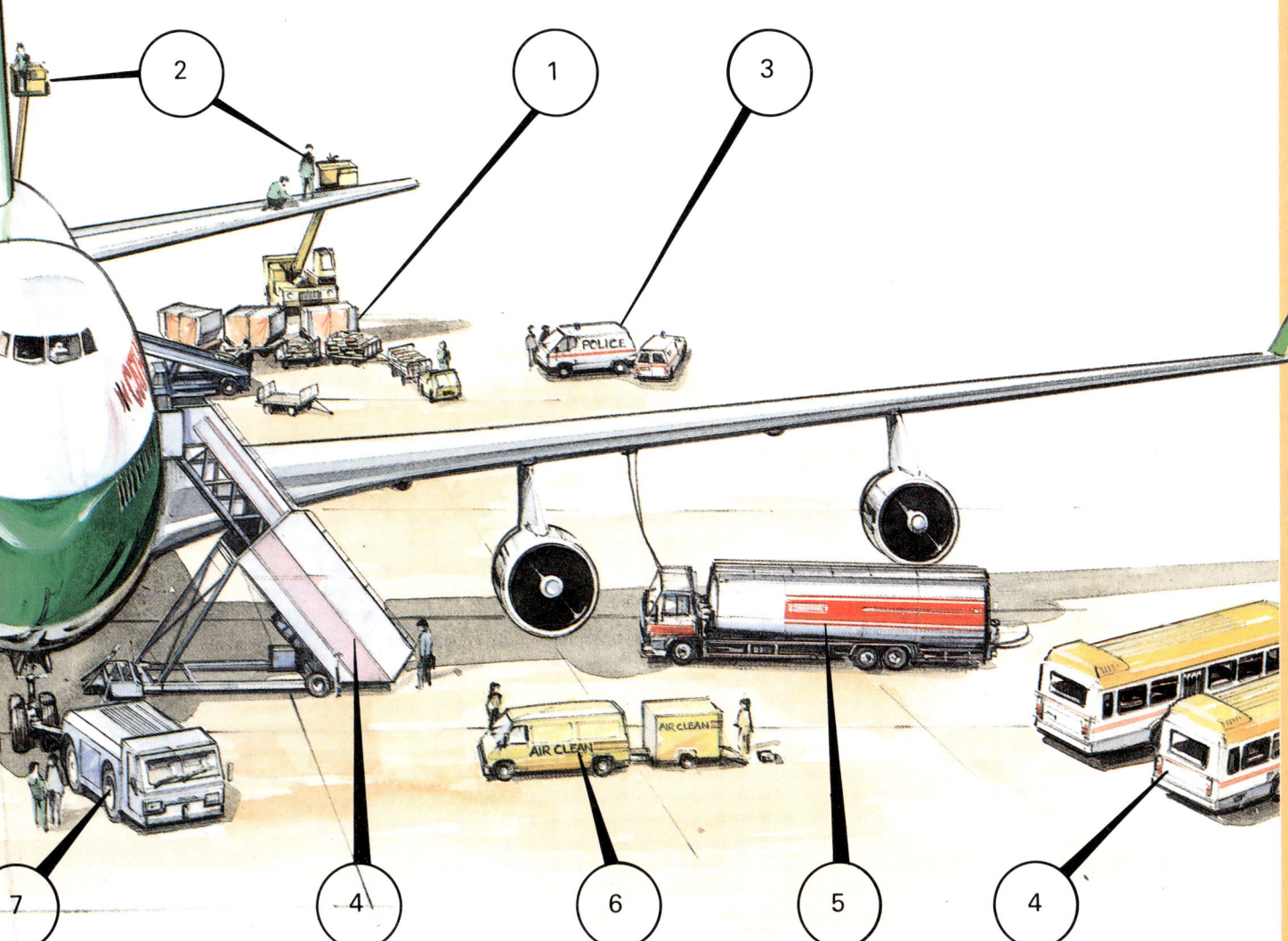

6 CABIN CLEANING
As soon as the last passenger is leaving the aircraft, the cleaners are boarding to remove the rubbish the passengers have left behind. Meanwhile a special vehicle plugs into an outlet in the aircraft to empty the toilets and washbasin wastes from the flight.

5 REFUELLING
Some airports have underground fuel pipes which lead to the aircraft parking positions. Fuel is either pumped via these points or from huge mobile tankers which fill up at the airport's own 'fuel farm'. A Boeing 747 can carry 215,000 litres (47,300 gallons) of fuel.

4 PASSENGER ENTRY/EXIT
Most modern airports have built piers with 'airbridges' which extend from the terminal to the aircraft door to provide a weather-proofed access. Otherwise passengers use airstairs and, if the distance is far enough, they are transported to and from the terminal by coach. Certain aircraft have their own integral stairs.

THE AIRPORT

Whatever glamorous image an airport might have, it is in fact little different from a bus or railway station. In the simplest terms, it is just another transport interchange, where people arrive by one form of transport (eg car or bus) and leave by another (aircraft). What makes an airport so exciting is that the passengers are travelling much further, often to foreign countries, and there is always the possibility of bumping into someone famous. For the people who work there, however, their job is just to help you on your way, as quickly and easily as possible.

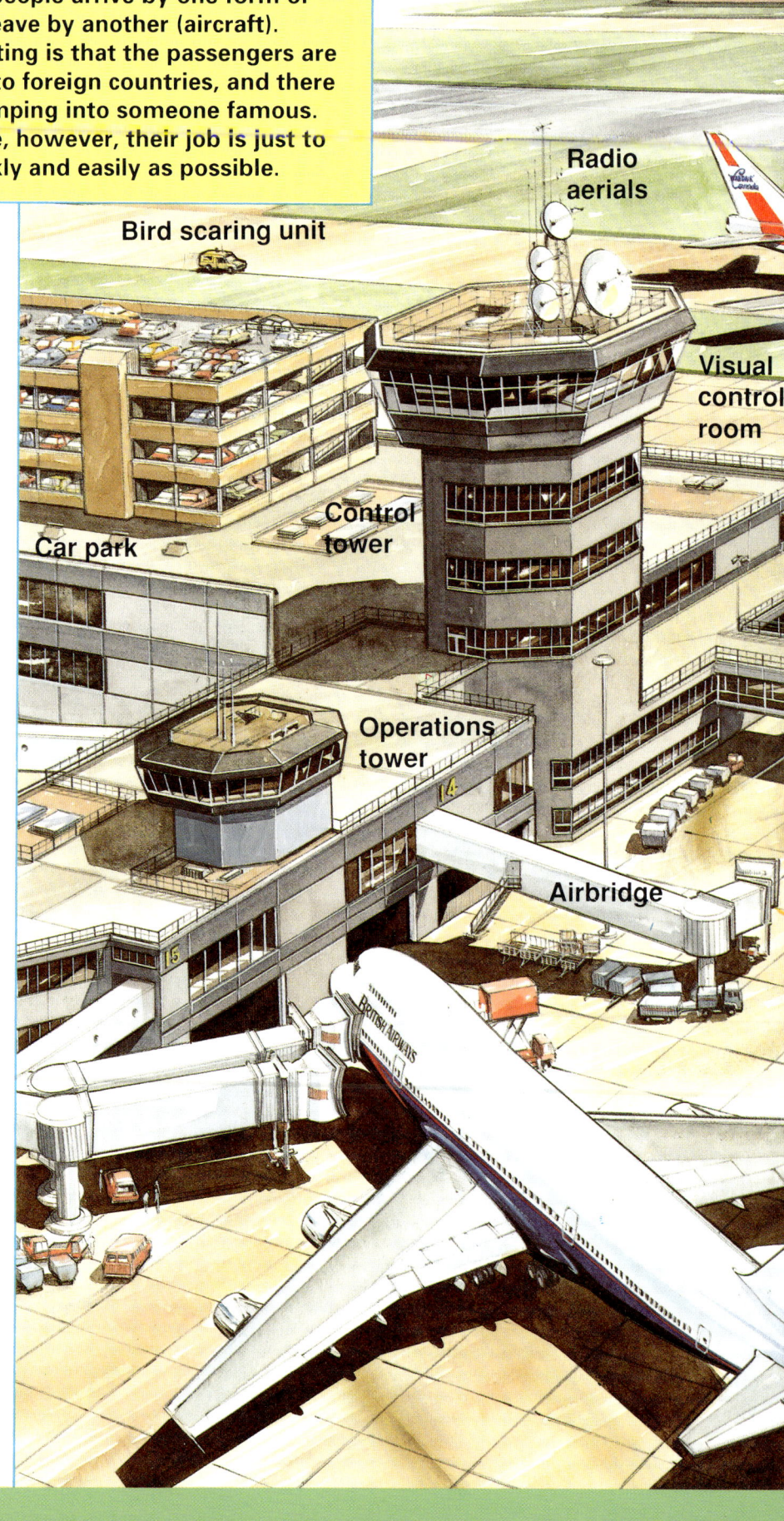

CONCOURSE
Between where passengers check in and where they pass through the security checks to go 'air side', there is a large area which contains shopping and refreshment facilities for passengers and their friends, and other services such as banking, car hire and conference rooms for businessmen.

SECURITY
It is an unfortunate fact that with the problems throughout the world, security at airports is all important. All passengers and their luggage are now searched by equipment which includes X-ray scanners and metal detection gates.

IMMIGRATION AND CUSTOMS
As flying is one of only two ways of leaving Britain (the other being sea), Customs and Excise and Immigration agencies are always present at an international airport. They are there to keep a watch to see if anyone is attempting to smuggle contraband or illegally enter or leave the country.

DEPARTURE LOUNGE
The departure lounge is provided for passengers who have checked in for their flight and passed through the security check. The lounge offers similar facilities to the concourse, although on a smaller scale, but for international flights includes duty and tax free shopping.

DUTY FREE SHOP
Every country sets its own levels of tax and duty on goods such as perfume, tobacco, wines and spirits. However, international agreements mean that passengers can buy a limited quantity of these items without paying tax or duty, but only if they buy them to use in a different country.

GATE POSITION
When the airline is ready to load the passengers, they call them to the place from which they will board the aircraft (the 'gate'). In most cases, the aircraft will be in sight on the apron adjacent to the gate position. Sometimes, a coach will be waiting there to take the passengers to a 'remote stand' where the aircraft is parked.

BAGGAGE RECLAIM
Arriving passengers follow a direct route which, on international flights, takes them through Immigration Control where they show their passports before collecting their luggage. Domestic passengers go straight to a separate baggage claim area to collect their luggage.

CUSTOMS
Every passenger who has arrived from a foreign country has to pass through a customs check to make sure that they are only bringing items into this country which are legally allowed or, where duty or tax are payable, the correct money is paid.

ARRIVAL HALL/MEETING POINT
When passengers have completed the inbound checks, they pass through to the arrivals hall where they can be met by friends, relatives or business contacts. There are facilities here for the traveller with no one to greet him, such as car hire and hotel reservations.

ON THE FLIGHT DECK

Over the years since the first airliners took to the skies, designs changed dramatically as designers learnt more about the secrets of flight. In recent years, the emphasis has changed as today's designers, having refined the aerodynamics, turned their attention to what happens inside an aircraft. To save weight (and therefore increase lift), aircraft are being designed and built using carbon fibre which is much lighter and stronger than traditional metals. The biggest change has been on how an airliner is 'driven'. In the past the flying controls were linked with the pilot's control column by a series of steel cables, rods and hinges, while he had rows of dials, lights and switches to monitor his flight. The Airbus A320 is the first of a new generation of airliners using 'fly by wire' and the 'glass cockpit' instead.

AUTOLAND CONTROL
To enable the pilot to make automatic landings in poor visibility.

STANDBY SYSTEMS
Traditional 'clock' instruments, including speed and altitude indicators, backing up the main electronic instruments.

FLY BY WIRE
The traditional control column ('joy stick') is being superseded by the side stick control. The slightest movement is detected by a computer which translates the information to make the relevant adjustment of the flight controls.

BRAKE LEVER

PILOT AND CO-PILOT POSITIONS
Today's airliners, including the 412-seat Boeing 747-400, have been designed to operate with just a two man crew, as against three or more in the past. This is because of more reliable equipment and better designed flight deck layouts which reduce the workload.

OVERHEAD PANEL
Hydraulic and electrical systems control panel and fuel management.

FLIGHT CONTROL UNIT
To dial in required heading, speed, altitude and vertical speed.

ENGINE AND WARNING DISPLAYS
These were once monitored by the flight engineer who sat by a special panel behind the co-pilot.

PRIMARY FLIGHT DISPLAY
This electronic display shows the crew the flight data, including speed, altitude and artificial horizon.

NAVIGATION DISPLAY
Another electronic display, it gives information on all navigational data, including radio beacons and flight plans.

RUDDER PEDALS
Used for turning the aircraft in flight.

SYSTEMS DISPLAY
With the engine and warning displays, this forms part of the electronic centralized aircraft monitoring (ECAM) system.

THROTTLES
Each lever controls the power of one of the engines. The thrust is increased as the levers are pushed forwards.

FLAPS AND SLATS LEVER
For extending both the flaps and slats to set angles.

19

THE FLIGHT

There is always a thrill when boarding an airliner, knowing that soon it will be taking off and heading to its destination. Often, where an airport has airbridges, the first time the passenger realizes that he has reached his aircraft is when he steps aboard! Behind the scenes, the cabin crews have been preparing the aircraft and now invite the passengers aboard. The pilot signs the load sheet and they are ready to go – once they get permission from the control tower. Throughout the flight, the flight and cabin crews will have little time to rest as they look after the aircraft and the passengers. It's only on the long distance flights that the crew have a few minutes to themselves.

PUSH BACK
Once the crew have completed their pre-flight checks, permission for starting the engines and leaving the stand is requested from the control tower. Most aircraft are parked 'nose in' to the terminal building or pier so that they take up as little space as possible. This means they have to be pushed back from the building before they can taxi to the runway.

TAXIING
Each taxiway has its own identity so that the controller can tell the pilot which route to take to get to the runway in use. Taxiways are connected to the runway by 'turn offs' which are also identified. When the final cockpit checks have taken place, the pilot asks the controller for permission to take off.

RUNWAY
The runway at a big airport can be over 2 miles (3.2 km) long, 150 ft (45 m) wide and built to take the impact of 350 tons (355 tonnes) of airliner landing every few minutes. Each runway is given a number which corresponds to the first two digits of the direction it faces (eg if this is 240°, it is known as runway 24). The direction in which the pilot takes off depends on which way the wind is blowing.

TAKE-OFF
As part of his pre-flight calculations, the pilot works out not just his route, but his take-off speed. This is based on a number of factors such as the weight of the aircraft, weather conditions and the length of the runway. When the throttle levers are pushed forward to reach the required engine power, the co-pilot calls out the calculated speeds as they are reached.

AUTOPILOT
As the aircraft climbs, the crew retract the undercarriage and the flaps and set the autopilot to guide them on their way. The autopilot will fly the aircraft at the height, speed and direction instructed by the flight crew. As the engines use up the fuel, the weight is reduced which means that the aircraft can be climbed, step by step, to maintain the most efficient fuel burn. This is known as cruise climb.

IN-FLIGHT ENTERTAINMENT

Although flying is fun for nearly everyone, a long flight can still be boring. Most airlines offer passengers films, videos and music channels to help them while away the hours. One airline has even provided live entertainment.

CABIN CREW

The cabin crew have a very busy time looking after the passengers' needs. Having made sure that everyone is in their seats with seat belts fastened, they close and lock the cabin doors. By law, they have to demonstrate the safety equipment to the passengers in case of emergency. In flight they serve meals and drinks and help passengers whenever called upon to do so.

APPROACH TO LAND

As the aircraft approaches its destination, the crew receive clearance from ATC to start their descent. As the aircraft is guided towards the runway, the crew keep a constant watch for other aircraft in the area. Meanwhile, the cabin crew tidy away empty trays and glasses and anything else that's loose, and make sure all the passengers are wearing their seat belts.

LANDING

The flight crew complete their final landing checks as the aircraft approaches the runway, adjust the flaps and throttle settings and lower the undercarriage. With the help of the Instrument Landing System (ILS) for accurate guidance, the aircraft touches down on the runway and is slowed down, often with reverse thrust.

PARKING

As the aircraft parks, the auxiliary power unit (APU) is started to provide power when the main engines are shut down. To ensure accurate parking, the pilot lines up the aircraft with a set of lights. The brakes are then applied and the final cockpit checks completed. In the passenger cabin, the doors are opened and the passengers leave the aircraft – which is then prepared for its next flight!

AIR TRAFFIC CONTROL

With so many aircraft crowding our skies, the airspace has been organized into an aerial road system, complete with junctions and traffic lights. The United Kingdom airspace is divided into two Flight Information Regions (FIRs) – London and Scottish – with air traffic control centres at West Drayton near London and Prestwick in Scotland. The Oceananic Area Control Centre, also at Prestwick, looks after aircraft crossing the North Atlantic to and from North America. The Flight Information Regions are divided up into Controlled and Uncontrolled Airspace. Aircraft flying in controlled airspace must be fitted with the correct navigation and communications equipment while the pilots must be qualified to operate under air traffic control instructions.

AIR TRAFFIC CONTROL

There are actually three different sections which go to make up Air Traffic Control. Area Control provides aircraft separation in controlled and special rules airspace. The controllers work in darkened rooms to make it easier to see their radar screens. Approach Control works from the control tower and guides the aircraft arriving and departing. Aerodrome Control, situated in the top of the control tower, looks after aircraft landing and taking off and all aircraft and vehicles moving about the airport.

RADAR

There are two types of radar. Primary radar provides basic information, showing the position of the aircraft. Secondary radar 'interrogates' the aircraft and provides extra information if the aircraft is fitted with a transponder. This information, which shows on the screen, can include the aircraft's identity, height, speed and destination.

NAVIGATION AIDS

The United Kingdom has a network of some one hundred stations for navigational aids. They provide radio signals for aircraft and indicate positions, including airports. There are three main types, VOR (VHF Omni-directional Range), DME (Distance Measuring Equipment) and NDB (Non-Directional Beacon).

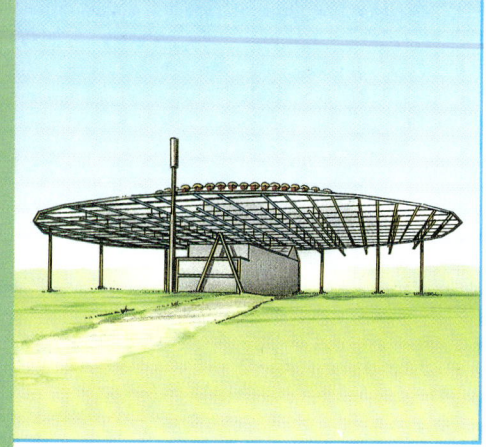

PHONETIC ALPHABET

To make sure that pilots and controllers don't mishear information, the letters of the alphabet have been given names. For example, if an aircraft has the identity G-SMCD, the pilot will contact ATC "This is Golf Sierra Mike Charlie Delta".

A	ALPHA	O	OSCAR
B	BRAVO	P	PAPA
C	CHARLIE	Q	QUEBEC
D	DELTA	R	ROMEO
E	ECHO	S	SIERRA
F	FOXTROT	T	TANGO
G	GOLF	U	UNIFORM
H	HOTEL	V	VICTOR
I	INDIA	W	WHISKY
J	JULIET	X	X-RAY
K	KILO	Y	YANKEE
L	LIMA	Z	ZULU
M	MIKE		
N	NOVEMBER		

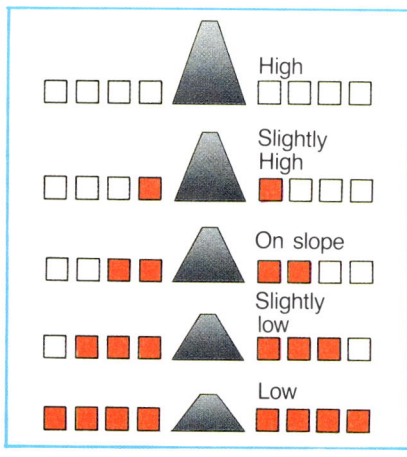

PAPI

A visual aid to let the pilot know when he is approaching the runway at the right angle is called the Precision Approach Path Indicator (PAPI). It consists of a series of high intensity light boxes alongside the runway which, depending on the combination of red and white lights, tell him if he is above, below or on the correct glide path.

THE UK AIRWAYS SYSTEM

Controlled airspace is divided into Control Zones which surround major airports, Terminal Control Areas (TMAs) which are usually where the airways meet near a major airport and Airways, which are the roads in the sky. These are corridors of space 10 miles (16 km) wide, stretching from 5,000 – 7,000 ft (1,500 – 2,500 m) up to 24,500 ft (7,350 m).

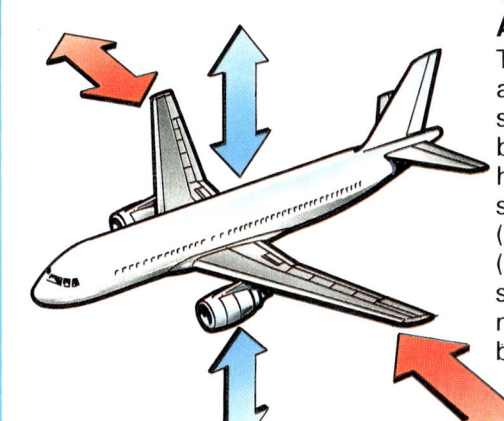

AIRCRAFT SEPARATION

The reason for creating airways is to keep aircraft separated from each other, both vertically and horizontally. The vertical separation is at least 1,000 ft (300 m) up to 29,000 ft (8,700 m) while horizontal separation is a minimum of 5 miles (8 km) when radar is being used.

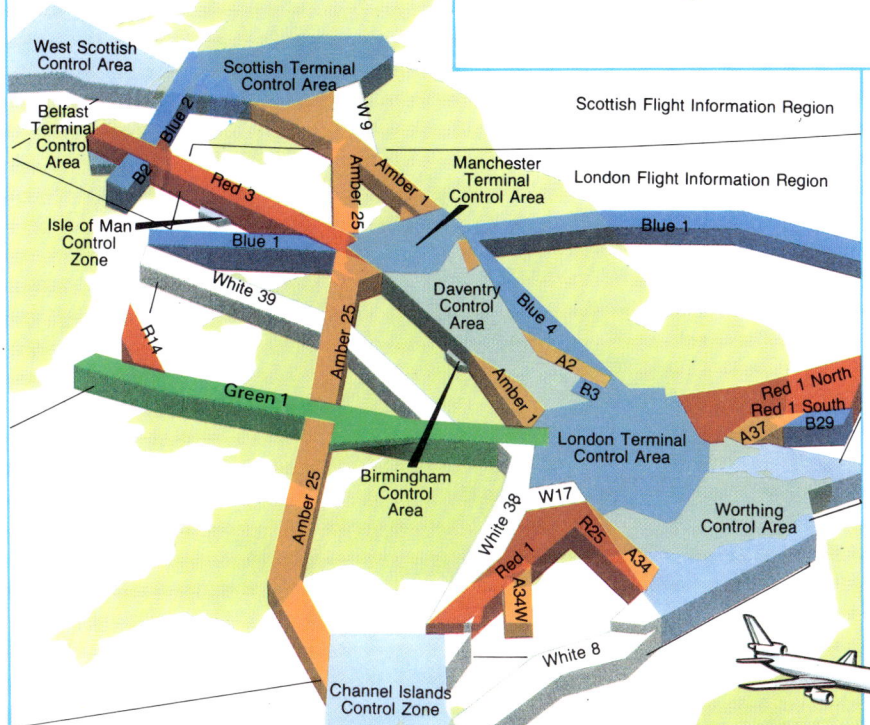

HOLDING SYSTEM

When an airport becomes very busy or the weather is too bad for a landing, aircraft are directed to a holding area, or stack. The pilot flies a special circuit around a radio beacon where each aircraft is vertically separated by at least 1,000 ft (300 m). As each aircraft is directed in to land from the bottom of the stack, the others drop to the next level down until it is their turn to land.

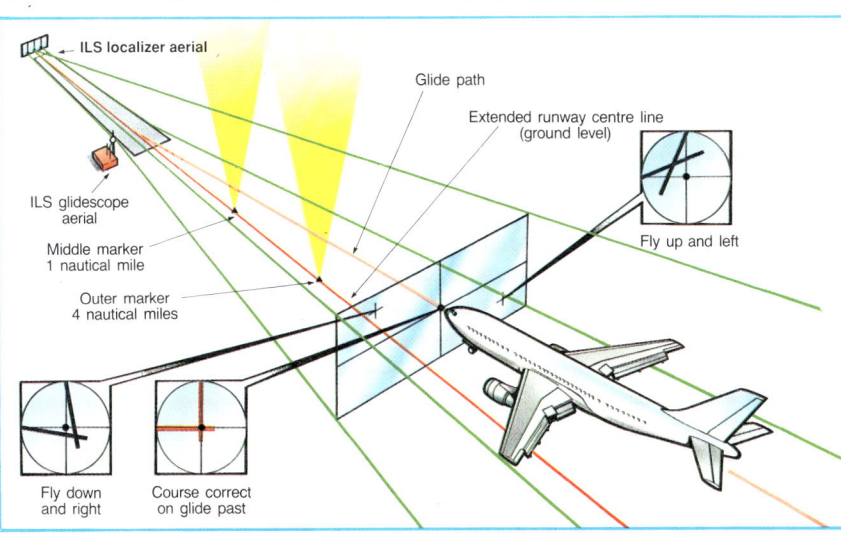

▲ Beacon

AUTOMATIC LANDING

The development of the Instrument Landing System (ILS) has made it possible for aircraft fitted with the right equipment to make automatic landings in poor visibility. The system uses two radio beams: the localizer, which defines the centreline of the runway and extends for about 20 miles (32 km), and the glide path, which defines the angle of approach for the aircraft.

23

MAINTENANCE AND ENGINEERING

A modern airliner is one of the most complex items of technology in use today. However, we are so used to seeing aircraft flying overhead, and even flying in them ourselves, that we tend to take air travel for granted. But, like the family car, aircraft and their engines must be serviced at regular intervals to ensure that everything is working properly and that they are safe to fly. Unlike cars, however, aircraft spend some 12 hours a week undergoing maintenance. Because aircraft have so many parts, it is not surprising that some items fail during a flight. In most cases they are not very important (eg a broken ashtray) and the repair can wait if necessary. To look after these requirements, airlines have maintenance bases where they service and maintain their aircraft fleet. In addition, they have a separate section which is responsible for sorting out faults reported by the pilot that must be dealt with immediately. Even though maintenance work is carried out in large hangars, it tends to be away from the passenger areas which means that the work, though vital, goes unnoticed.

LINE MAINTENANCE

Every aircraft has a technical log which contains details of any faults which develop during a flight. Before they land, the flight crew radio ahead with details of the faults which are then rectified by the line maintenance engineers during turn-round. Some faults have to be fixed otherwise the aircraft will not be allowed to depart, while others can wait until the next base check.

MAINTENANCE BAYS

The hangar is divided into bays, which makes the maximum use of the floor area. Long term work will be put in bays furthest from the hangar doors so that other aircraft can be brought in and sent out without having to disrupt the work.

MAINTENANCE CHECKS

Because of the commercial need to keep aircraft flying, while at the same time making sure they are safe to operate, a number of maintenance procedures have been adopted by the aircraft manufacturers and the airlines. They range from a check after every 100 flying hours (check the lubrication, filters, etc.) to the major check where the aircraft is completely stripped down (which can take two weeks).

STORES

To save valuable time when parts need to be replaced, the airline has its own stores section which holds essential stocks from aircraft tyres to electrical fuses. It would not be possible, or practical, to hold every possible part so it is the section's responsibility to order special parts as they are required.

MAINTENANCE HANGAR

In the same way as cars are serviced under cover in garages, aircraft are towed into a hangar for maintenance work. While traditional hangars might cover an area of some 5000 ft^2 (465 m^2) with doors 25 ft (7.6 m) high, modern hangars designed for wide body airliners can cover more than three times the space and reach a height of 70 ft (21.4 m).

CONVERSION WORK

As aircraft go through life, designers work on the original plans and improve and adapt them to achieve better performance or carry out different roles. These can be reasonably small jobs or major projects (see the Super Guppy, page 29).

THE PAINT SHOP

For various reasons such as age or the airline adopting a new livery, aircraft need to be repainted during their lifespan. This is a specialist job using paints developed to take the rigours of flying. To protect other workers and the spread of the paint from the pneumatic paint guns, the paint bay is curtained off from the rest of the hangar.

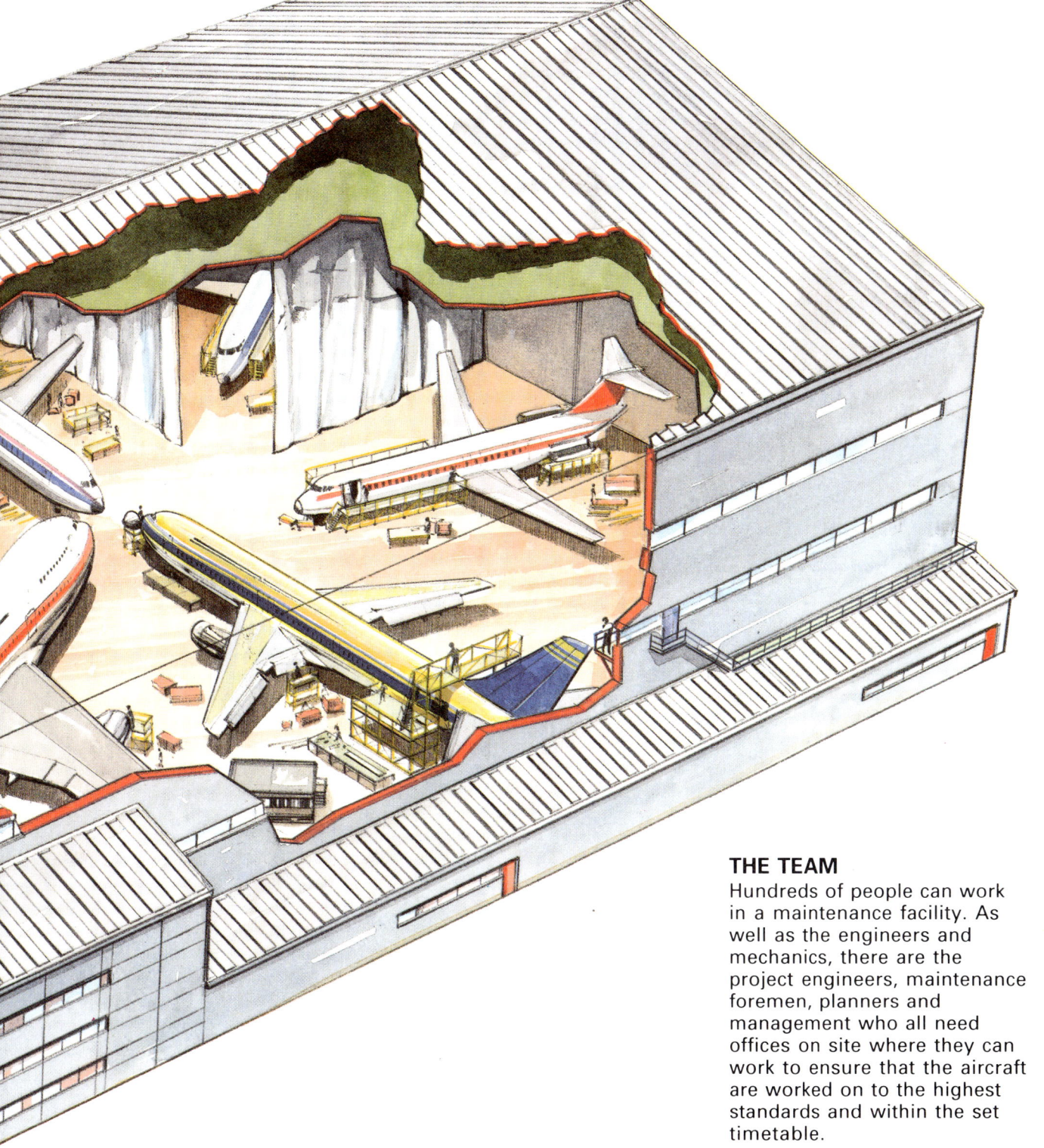

THE TEAM

Hundreds of people can work in a maintenance facility. As well as the engineers and mechanics, there are the project engineers, maintenance foremen, planners and management who all need offices on site where they can work to ensure that the aircraft are worked on to the highest standards and within the set timetable.

AIRLINES AND AIRCRAFT

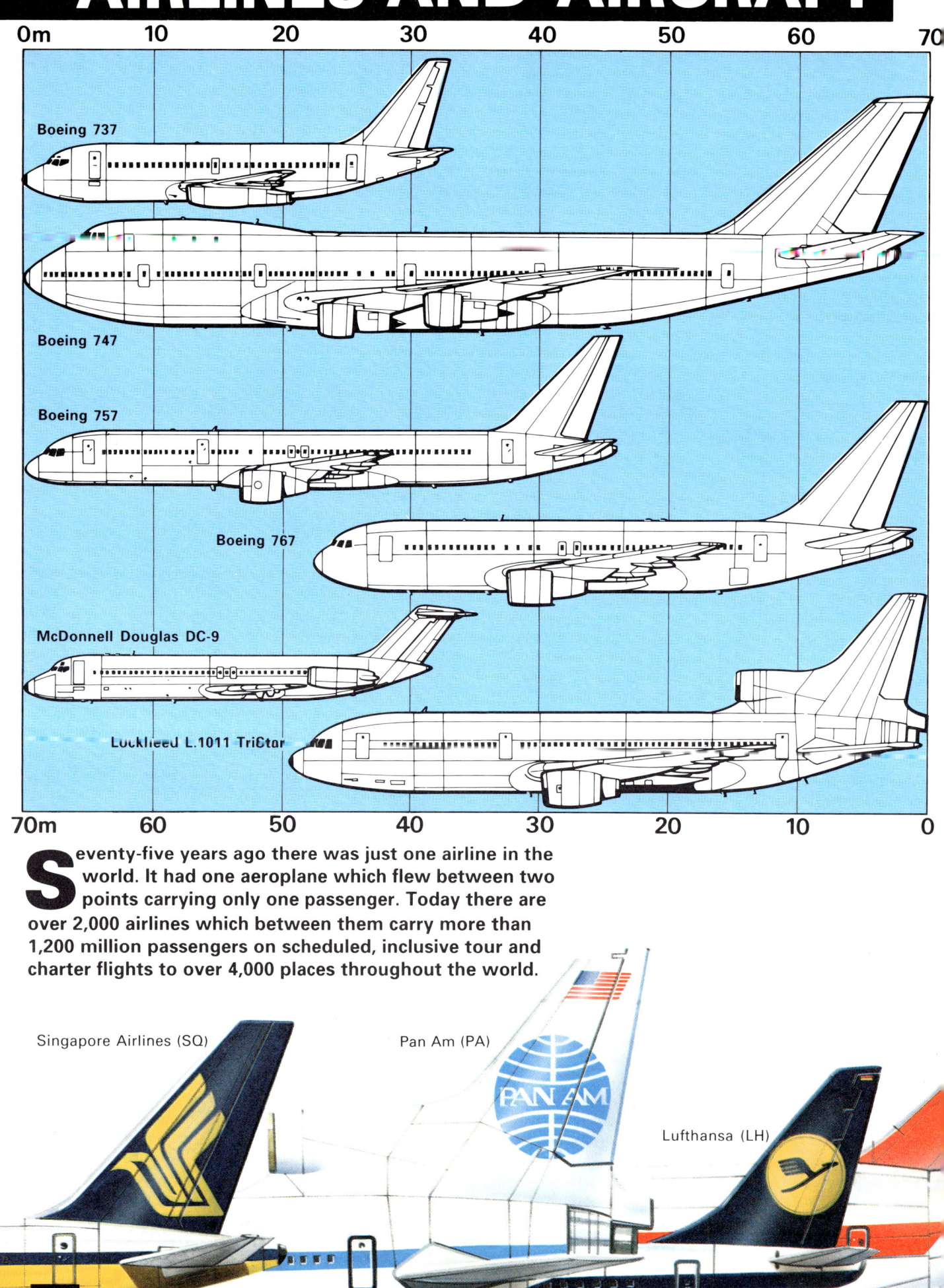

Seventy-five years ago there was just one airline in the world. It had one aeroplane which flew between two points carrying only one passenger. Today there are over 2,000 airlines which between them carry more than 1,200 million passengers on scheduled, inclusive tour and charter flights to over 4,000 places throughout the world.

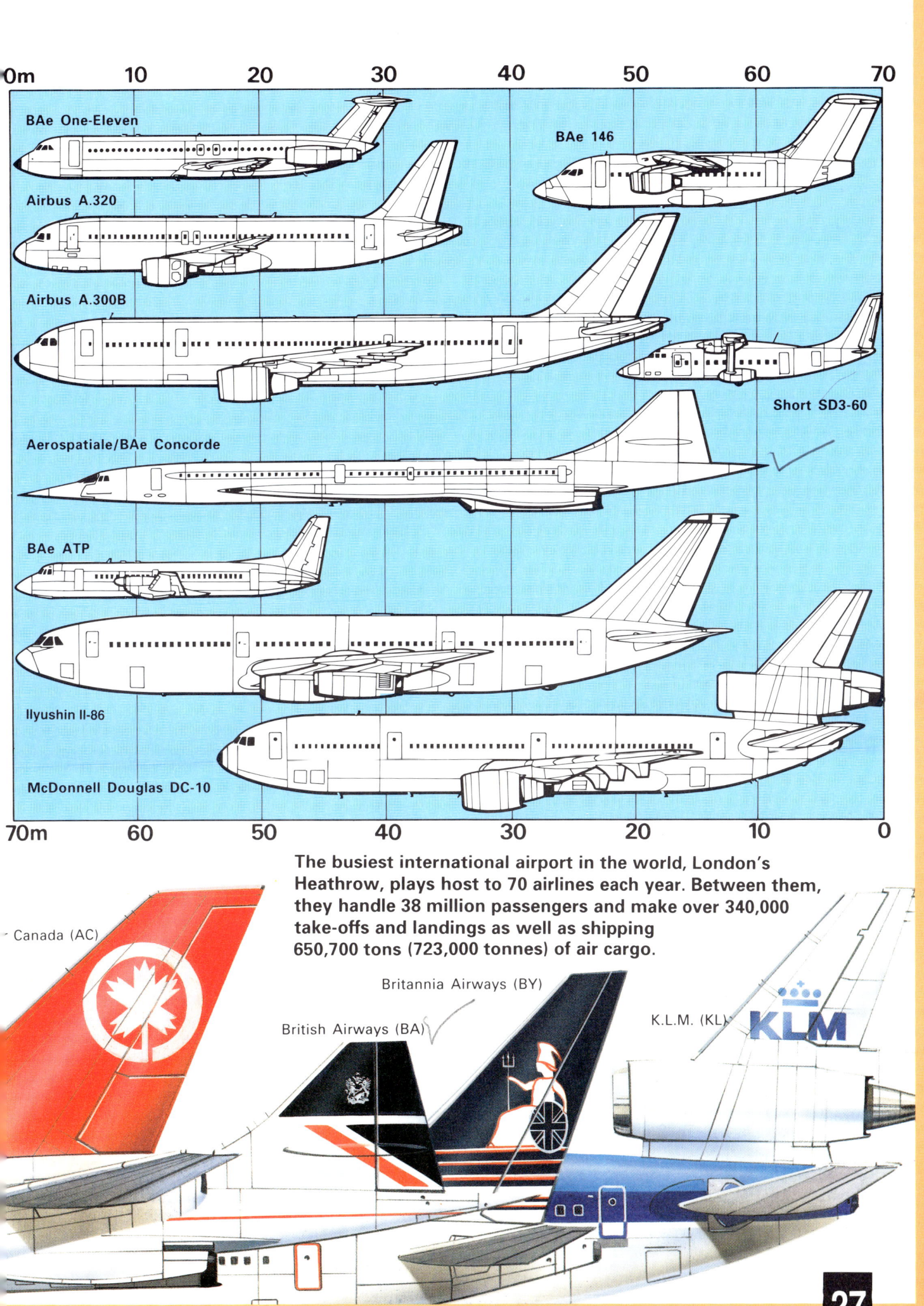

CARGO

Cargo has always been the poor relation of the air transport industry. Not only does it not have the glamour of passenger flying, but much of it is flown at night. Many flights are by aircraft which have special 'quick change' interiors which means that they operate passenger flights during the day and, with the seats removed and the interior wall panels protected, fly freight at night. The introduction of wide body airliners with their large underfloor holds has greatly increased the space available for cargo. Unlike other forms of transport, cargo accounts for only a very small portion of total revenue. Even so, it is not unusual for an international airport to handle over 4 million lbs (2 million kg) of cargo a week (worth over £2 million per day).

CHARTER FLIGHTS

A lot of cargo travels on special charter flights, especially for unusual or outsize items where speed is vital and for consignments to developing parts of the world. The CL-44 is a specially designed cargo aircraft which has a swing tail to enable larger loads to be carried.

AIR CARGO CENTRE

Specialized air cargo centres are designed to bring together everyone involved, including the airlines, bonded warehouses, Customs and Excise, freight agents, forwarders, consolidators, brokers and transporters, in one self-contained unit. Freight is transferred to and from landside and airside, from truck to aircraft.

CONTAINERIZATION

In order to speed up turn-round times, cargo is containerized before the aircraft arrives. The containers, which are specially shaped to fit inside the fuselage, are loaded using a scissor lift. Both the lift and the cabin floor are fitted with rollers so the containers can be easily pushed into position by hand.

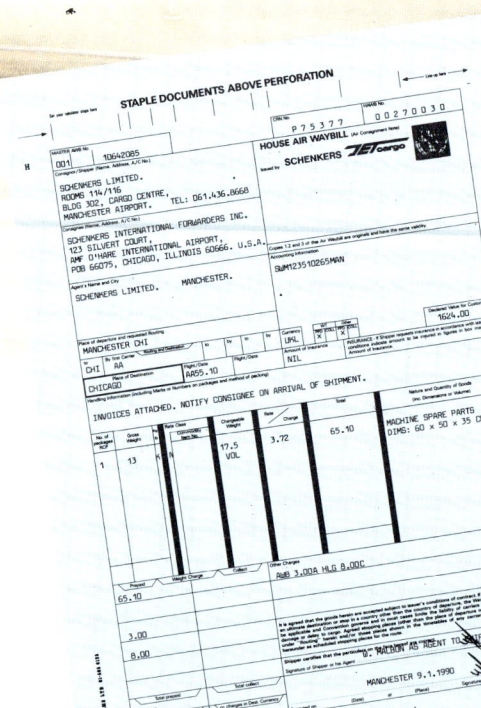

SUPER GUPPY

Some aircraft are modified so much that little of the original design remains. The Super Guppy is a conversion of the Boeing C-97 military transport which was developed to support the US space

programme. Four aircraft were converted for Airbus Industrie and can be seen at some UK airports collecting Airbus wings for final assembly in Toulouse, France.

ANYTHING GOES

While it is not profitable to send certain goods by air because they have a low value in relation to their bulk (eg potatoes), the variety and oddity of some items that can be found in freight holds is surprising. They include precious stones, aircraft engines, tropical fish, newspapers, eggs, funeral caskets, ships' propellers, flowers and fashion clothes.

AIR WAYBILL

All air freight must be accompanied by a document called an air waybill. As well as being the agreement between the shipper and the carrier, it also serves other uses, such as customs import and export clearance and as a receipt for both shipment and delivery.

ROYAL MAIL

Mail is very important to airlines, which have to be specially registered as a carrier. Certain airports are used as hubs for the Royal Mail postal service. At these points, mail arrives during the night when it is sorted for onward delivery to the hub airport nearest its final destination.

GLOSSARY

AEROPLANE – A fixed wing, heavier than air powered flying machine.

AILERON – A flap hinged to the rear edge of the wing used for rolling the aircraft.

AIRBRIDGE – A moveable covered walkway connecting the pier with the aircraft entrance.

AIRCRAFT – Any machine that can fly by means of aerodynamic forces or buoyancy, eg aeroplane, glider or helicopter.

AIR CREW – The people on duty on board an aircraft, consisting of flight crew and cabin crew.

AIRFIELD – A designated area for aircraft movements.

AIRFRAME – The body of an aircraft, excluding its engines and systems.

AIR INTAKE – The entrance for air passing into the engine.

AIRLINER – A large passenger aircraft.

AIRPORT – A place with runways and passenger facilities where civil aircraft operate.

AIRSIDE – The parts of an airport under the control of Customs and Immigration.

AIRSPEED INDICATOR – An instrument which shows the speed of the aircraft relative to the air through which it moves.

AIR TRAFFIC CONTROL (ATC) – A system of regional centres and airport units which instruct aircraft which height, speed and direction they must fly.

AIRWAY – A fixed air route, equipped with navigational aids.

ALTIMETER – An instrument which shows the aircraft's height above sea or ground level.

APPROACH – The path taken by an aircraft coming into land.

APPROACH CONTROL – The section of ATC that directs a flight during its approach to land.

APRON – The hard standing in front of the terminal building, piers and hangars.

AUTOMATIC PILOT – A device that automatically steers an aircraft on a preset course.

AUXILIARY POWER UNIT (APU) – A small jet engine built into an aircraft to provide power on the ground when the main engines are shut down (eg for air conditioning).

BOARDING CARD – A document given to the passenger at check-in confirming he can embark on his flight.

CABIN – The part of the fuselage where the passengers sit.

CABIN CREW – The members of the air crew who look after the passengers.

CHECK-IN – The place at an airport where a passenger registers for a flight.

CHOCK – A small block placed at the wheels of a parked aircraft to stop it moving.

COCKPIT – The forward part of the aircraft which houses the pilot and his flight crew.

CONCOURSE – A large hall at an airport between check-in and the departure lounge containing shops and services for passengers and their friends.

CONTROL SURFACES – The moving parts of an aircraft used to steer, ie ailerons, elevators and rudder.

CONTROL TOWER – The building at an airport from which air traffic is controlled.

CUSTOMS AND EXCISE – The government department responsible for collecting duty on imported and exported goods.

DRAG – The force resisting the movement of an aircraft through the air.

ELEVATOR – A flap hinged to the rear of an aircraft's horizontal tail, making it climb or descend.

FIN – The vertical stabilizer at the rear of an aircraft.

FLAPS – Moving devices on the rear of the wings between the ailerons and the fuselage which increase lift on take-off and drag during landing.

FLAP SETTING – The angle at which the flaps are set to vary the lift or drag.

FLIGHT – The art or act of flying; a particular air service provided by an airline.

FLIGHT CREW – See air crew

FLIGHT DECK – See cockpit

FLIGHT NUMBER – A unique shorthand code consisting of an airline's flight code and a number which is used to define a particular flight.

FLIGHT RECORDER – A device that records information on an aircraft's performance in flight.

FUSELAGE – The main body of an aircraft to which the wings and tail are attached.

GATE – The position in an airport terminal from which passengers board their flight.

GROUND POWER UNIT – A portable generator which provides power to an aircraft when its engines are shut down.

HANGAR – A large building for housing aircraft undergoing maintenance or repair.

INCLUSIVE TOUR – A holiday package which includes the flight as well as the hotel in the price.

INSTRUMENT LANDING SYSTEM (ILS) – The standard landing aid which assists aircraft to land automatically in poor visibility.

LANDING GEAR – The assemblies of struts, shock absorbers and wheels that support an aircraft on the ground.

LANDSIDE – The part of an airport outside the control of the Customs and Immigration authorities.

LIFT – The upward force on an aircraft, opposing gravity.

LOAD SHEET – The document recording the various weights that go to make up an aircraft's total weight.

MACH NUMBER – The ratio of the airspeed of an aircraft to the speed of sound in the same conditions. Mach number 1 = the speed of sound.

MOVEMENT, AIRCRAFT – A take-off or a landing.

NOTAM (NOTICE TO AIRMEN) – A daily bulletin of aviation information for flight crews.

PIER – A covered extension from the airport terminal building incorporating gate positions from which passengers board their aircraft.

PISTON ENGINE (RECIPROCATING ENGINE) – An engine whose working parts (pistons) move up and down.

PROPELLER – Blades fixed to a central hub which are rotated by a piston engine or turboprop to produce thrust to propel an aircraft.

PUSH BACK – The action of reversing an aircraft away from its stand using a tug.

RADAR – Electronic equipment which can locate the position and height of an aircraft.

RECIPROCATING ENGINE – See piston engine

REVERSE THRUST – Jet engine power used in slowing down a landing run.

RUDDER – The vertical control surface attached to the rear of the fin used to steer the aircraft left or right.

RUNWAY – An area of ground from which aircraft take off and land.

SCHEDULED SERVICE – A regular passenger flight operated by an airline.

SLAT – A moveable aerofoil fixed to the leading edge of the wing to create extra lift.

SPEED OF SOUND – The speed at which sound travels through the air.

STAND – A parking space for an aircraft.

STILL AIR RANGE – The maximum distance an aircraft can fly if there is no wind.

TAXIWAY – A paved track connecting the runway with the apron areas.

THRUST – The force that propels an aircraft forward.

TOUCH DOWN – The moment when an aircraft's wheels meet the ground on landing.

TOWBAR – The connecting bar between a tug and the aircraft's nose undercarriage used for push back.

TURBOFAN – A bypass jet engine where the turbine drives a large fan to increase the thrust.

TURBOJET – A jet propelled gas turbine engine where the exhaust gases provide the thrust.

TURBOPROP – A jet engine in which the turbine is connected to a propeller which provides the thrust.

TURN-ROUND – The act of an aircraft arriving, unloading, reloading and departing.

UNDERCARRIAGE – See landing gear

YAW – To deviate in a horizontal direction from the line of flight.

AIRPORT CHECKLIST

Next time you travel on an aircraft keep a look out for some of the things mentioned in this book. Use the list below to record what you have seen. Don't worry if you don't see everything on your first trip. This will depend on the airline you are flying with and the size of the airport.

IN THE TERMINAL

Airbridge
Airline ticket
Arrivals hall
Arrivals information board
Baggage reclaim hall
Boarding card
Bus and coach station
Car hire desks
Car park courtesy coach
Check-in desk
Concourse
Conveyor belt
Customs hall
Customs officer
Departure gate
Departure hall
Departure information board
Domestic departure lounge
Duty-free shop
Foreign passport
Gift shop
Information desk
Luggage ticket
Meeting point
Metal detector gate
Passport control
Porter
Restaurant
Seat allocation chart
Security checkpoint
Taxi rank
Tour operator's desk
X-ray machine

ON THE APRON

Aircraft stand and number
Airline maintenance engineer
Airport police
Baggage handlers
Baggage trolley
Catering vehicle
Chocks
Crew bus
Fire vehicle
Flight dispatcher
Freight container
Fuel bowser
Ground power unit
Passenger steps
Sewage disposal vehicle
Tow bar
Tow truck
Water tanker

ON THE AIRFIELD

Cargo centre
Control tower
Fire station
Fuel depot
Hangar
Landing lights
Radar scanner
Runway
Taxiway

IN THE AIRLINER

Chief steward
Cockpit
Emergency exit
First officer
In-flight meal
In-flight video
Lavatory
Overhead locker
Pilot
Refreshments trolley
Safety signs
Seat belt

AIRCRAFT TYPES

Aerospatiale ATR-42
Airbus A.300
Airbus A.310
Airbus A.320
BAe ATP
BAe One-Eleven
BAe 146
BAe 748
Boeing 707
Boeing 727
Boeing 737
Boeing 747
Boeing 757
Boeing 767
Concorde
DC-8
DC-9
DC-10
Fokker F.27 Friendship
Ilyushin Il-62
Ilyushin Il-86
Lockheed TriStar
MD-80
Super Guppy
Tupolev Tu-134
Tupolev Tu-154